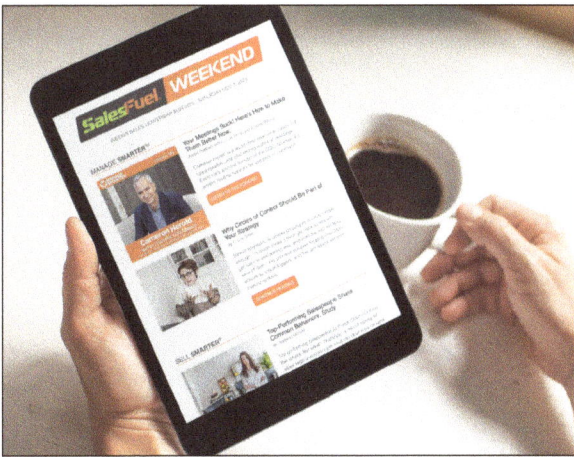

You can get fresh insights for building your sales credibility every Saturday with the SalesFuel Weekend newsletter. Free signup at https://salesfuel.com/newsletter

SalesCred™

How Buyers Qualify Sellers

C. Lee Smith

THiNK*aha*®

An Actionable Sales Journal

E-mail: info@thinkaha.com
20660 Stevens Creek Blvd., Suite 210
Cupertino, CA 95014

Please go to
https://aha.pub/SalesCred
to read this AHAbook and to share the
individual AHAmessages that resonate with you.

Published by THiNKaha®
20660 Stevens Creek Blvd., Suite 210,
Cupertino, CA 95014
https://thinkaha.com
E-mail: info@thinkaha.com

Second Printing: January 2021
First Printing: October 2020
Hardcover ISBN: 978-1-61699-381-8   1-61699-381-2
Paperback ISBN: 978-1-61699-380-1   1-61699-380-4
eBook ISBN: 978-1-61699-379-5   1-61699-379-0
Place of Publication: Silicon Valley, California, USA
Paperback Library of Congress Number: 2020917454

Introduction

In sales, there's a lot of talk about qualifying the buyer. What's the lead scoring say? Are they a marketing-qualified lead or a sales-qualified lead? Do they fit our ideal customer profile? Will they buy enough to become an enterprise account?

Perhaps you've gotten it exactly BACKWARD. Instead, you should be talking about how the buyer qualifies (and disqualifies) the seller. What determines whom they invite to compete for the business? Whom do they call or email back? And whom they share sensitive business information with?

How the buyer perceives the seller has significantly more impact on whether a sale is made than how the seller perceives the buyer. This is why having Sales Credibility is so vitally important.

Like the credentials pictured on the cover of this book, having SalesCred™ gives you access to important people and information that ordinary salespeople simply can't get.

A buyer is far more likely to honestly answer your discovery questions if you are known to help people solve problems, achieve goals, and improve their business results.

A top executive is far more likely to instruct the gatekeeper to schedule a meeting when they believe that you won't waste their time—and that associating with you won't come back to bite them later.

Yet most salespeople close these doors with the words they say and the actions they take every day, both online and in person. They give away their credibility, their leverage, their POWER, in a business relationship that is already tilted in favor of the buyer. But it doesn't have to be this way.

I believe that sales, when done right, is a noble profession, but the industry needs a framework to make it easier for salespeople to learn how to be credible. This book discusses that framework, which is represented in The Hierarchy of Sales Credibility pictured below. The hierarchy is based on the work I have been doing at my firm, SalesFuel, for more than thirty years.

THE HIERARCHY OF SALES CREDIBILITY

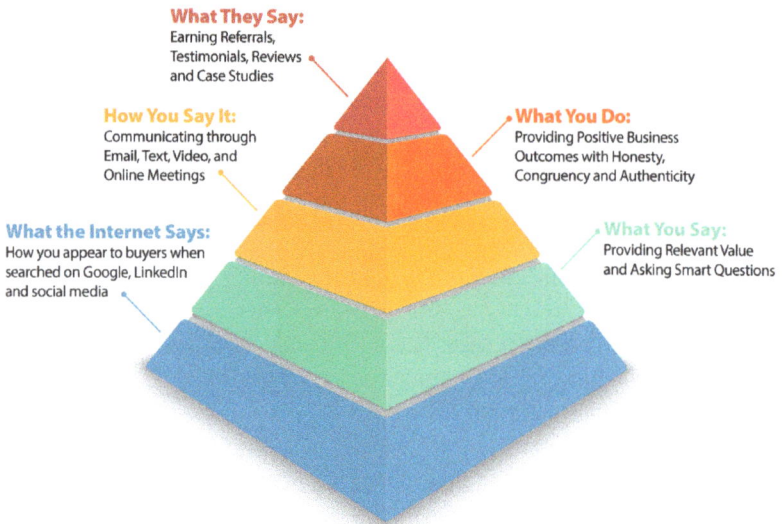

What They Say:
Earning Referrals,
Testimonials, Reviews
and Case Studies

How You Say It:
Communicating through
Email, Text, Video, and
Online Meetings

What You Do:
Providing Positive Business
Outcomes with Honesty,
Congruency and Authenticity

What the Internet Says:
How you appear to buyers when
searched on Google, LinkedIn
and social media

What You Say:
Providing Relevant Value
and Asking Smart Questions

Starting with the foundation of the pyramid and building upward allow you to achieve what all salespeople want: credibility through the perception of others in the form of referrals and testimonials.

This book explains The Hierarchy of Sales Credibility and how each layer builds upon the last, enabling you to reach ultimate sales credibility—when those who know you talk about you in a way that positively influences those who don't, which makes future sales much easier.

While I was writing this book, my publisher, Mitchell Levy, was at the tail end of interviewing 500 thought leaders on credibility. His work led to a number of outcomes, including a new definition of credibility, which he discusses in-depth in his book, *Credibility Nation*, and which you'll see in the Three Pillars of Credibility diagram in Chapter 1 of this book.

The Three Pillars of Credibility and The Hierarchy of Sales Credibility complement each other. In order to move up the pyramid to a higher level of credibility, you need to succeed at being known, being likeable, and being trustworthy in what you say and do.

Salespeople can use the tips in this book to learn how to move up the hierarchy. Sales managers can use the framework to grow their sales team and provide their team members with the necessary training and coaching to increase credibility.

My first book, *Hire Smarter, Sell More!*, helps sales managers understand how to use data and analytics to hire salespeople who can build credibility and add significant value while being team players (e.g., not being a toxic troublemaker).

This book benefits both buyers and sellers by increasing the credibility of sales professionals, based not on theory, but on proprietary research done with B2B buyers, sales managers, salespeople and top company executives. Supporting data appears throughout this book and in the Appendix.

As you read *SalesCred*, you will learn what sales credibility is about and how salespeople can live and work credibly. When you apply the knowledge gained from this book, you will see growth in your sales numbers and happiness in your life—and the lives of others you serve every day.

Dedication

I dedicate this book to the two most important women in my life.

To Kelly Smith, my wife, best friend, and the best sale I ever made. She spent numerous nights and weekends by my side to help me get my company started during our salad days. She also is the CEO of the Smith household and one of the hardest workers I've ever known.

To Audrey Strong, my second-best friend whom I've known since college. She shares my dedication to ridiculously high service levels. For ten years, she never had to solicit new clients for her PR firm. They all came to her by referral. Another one of my best sales was convincing her to join my firm, SalesFuel.

Acknowledgements

Special thanks to Kathy Crosett, Vice President of Research and one of the OGs at SalesFuel. Kathy and I collaborate on all of the primary research for the firm, including many of the findings contained in this book. She is one of the most credible people I know. I rarely publish anything without Kathy reviewing it first.

Special thanks to Mitchell Levy. He is not only my publisher but also the Global Credibility Expert and author of *Credibility Nation*, which focuses on how all humans can become more credible. Together, our two books will contribute toward setting a higher standard of public discourse and professional conduct in the world. I truly enjoyed the brainstorming sessions we've had on both books, as well as his guidance on presenting the SalesCred story.

Special thanks to Tyler Welsh for his commitment to excellence as Creative Manager at SalesFuel. Tyler created the graphics for this book.

A THiNKaha book is not your typical book. It's a whole lot more while being a whole lot less. Scan the QR code or use this link to watch me talk about this new evolutionary style of book: https://aha.pub/THiNKahaSeries

How to Read a THiNKaha® Book
A Note from the Publisher

The AHAthat/THiNKaha series was crafted to deliver content the way humans process information in today's world. Short, sweet, and to the point while delivering powerful, lasting impact.

The content is designed and presented in ways to appeal to visual, auditory, and kinesthetic personality types. Each section contains AHA messages, lines for notes, and a meme that summarizes that section. You should also scan the QR code, or click on the link, to watch a video of the author talking about that section.

This book is contextual in nature. Although the words won't change, their meaning will every time you read it as your context will. Be ready, you will experience your own AHA moments as you read. The AHA messages are designed to be stand-alone actionable messages that will help you think differently. Items to consider as you're reading include:

1. It should only take less than an hour to read the first time. When you're reading, write one to three action items that resonate with you in the underlined areas.
2. Mark your calendar to re-read it again.
3. Repeat step #1 and mark one to three additional AHA messages that resonate. As they will most likely be different, this is a great time to reflect on the messages that resonated with you during your last reading.
4. Sprinkle credust on the author and yourself by sharing the AHA messages from this book socially from the AHAthat platform https://aha.pub/SalesCred.

After reading this THiNKaha book, marking your AHA messages, rereading it, and marking more AHA messages, you'll begin to see how this book contextually applies to you. We advocate for continuous, lifelong learning and this book will help you transform your AHAs into action items with tangible results.

Mitchell Levy, Global Credibility Expert
publisher@thinkaha.com

THiNKaha®

Contents

3 PILLARS of
CREDIBILITY

Being Known

Demonstrating your desire to serve others.

Showing your intent.

Demonstrating your commitment.

Sharing your integrity.

Being Likeable

Sharing your "stage."

Showing respect by "showing up when you show up."

Being Trustworthy

Showing up as your authentic self.

Demonstrating integrity in all you say and do.

Showing your vulnerability.

Being coachable in every situation.

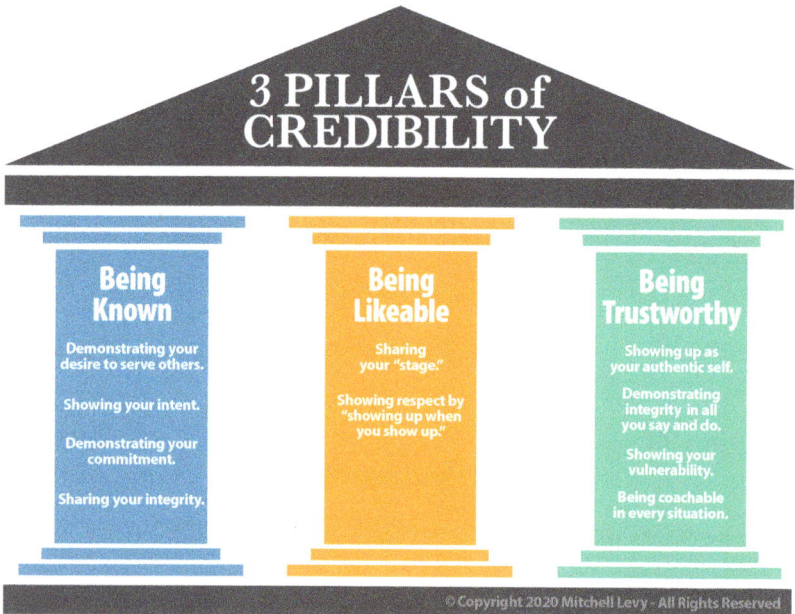

Credibility, as defined by Mitchell Levy in his book, Credibility Nation, requires being known, being likeable, and being trustworthy. It is much more than just having integrity or being friendly. In fact, if one pillar crumbles, so does one's credibility.

Share the AHA messages from this book socially by going to https://aha.pub/SalesCred.

Section I

Introduction

Only 1 in 4 North Americans views salespeople as credible in what they say and do, according to The State of Credibility survey conducted in September 2020 by SalesFuel®, Credibility Nation™, and Behavioral Resource Group. The number is even lower for automotive salespeople. 1 in 3 adults view real estate agents as credible.

Credibility is the pre-requisite of trust. A high degree of credibility is required for a salesperson to gain access to top decision-makers, sensitive business information, and the leverage needed to close business. Every word and action taken by salespeople, at all stages of the sales process, should boost your credibility, enabling you to earn the buyer's trust.

The major problem is that most salespeople unknowingly limit their success by pushing their prospects away with the words they speak and the actions they take every day.

This section discusses what sales credibility is and how valuable it is for salespeople to have and to build. By understanding credibility and the role it plays in sales, sales managers can be more effective in guiding their salespeople toward success.

Scan the QR code or use this link to watch the section videos and more on this section topic:
https://aha.pub/SalesCresSVs

1

Credibility is the master key that unlocks the sales process. Every stage, whether it be connecting, discovery, solving, or closing, becomes much easier when your prospect perceives you as credible.
#SalesCred
http://cleesmith.com

_____

_____

_____

2

Most salespeople want to be thought of as "trusted advisors." But you cannot be trusted without a high degree of credibility. #SalesCred https://cleesmith.com

_____

_____

_____

3

A salesperson without credibility is not only at a competitive disadvantage today, they're at risk for being replaced by AI tomorrow. #SalesCred http://cleesmith.com

_____

_____

_____

4

All sales managers want to have a high-performing sales team. To achieve this goal, they have to improve both their sales process and their salespeople. Building credibility is a rare opportunity to do both at the same time. https://salescred.com

---

5

Credibility is being known, being likable, and being trustworthy. It is one of the basic foundations of building good relationships,which is the essence of sales. #SalesCred https://mitchelllevy.com/credibility —Mitchell Levy

---

6

Being Known includes impacting customers in positive ways and letting other people know about it. Ideally, they'll hear it from the customer. http://cleesmith.com

_____

_____

_____

7

What are you known for? What do you WANT to be known for by your clients and prospects? What is your area of expertise that rises above your competition? What are you doing to BECOME known? #SalesCred http://cleesmith.com

_____

_____

_____

8

Being Likable is more than being friendly, happy, and successful. It's about sharing credit for your successes and showing the expected level of respect for other people and things.
#SalesCred http://cleesmith.com

9

Being Trustworthy is a key requirement of a credible salesperson. Anything you say or do that the buyer believes to be untrustworthy immediately kills your credibility. #SalesCred https://aha.pub/MitchellLevy

---

10

#SalesCred requires follow-through, accountability, and congruence. Always deliver what you promised. Admit your mistakes. What you say and what you do must always be in alignment. http://cleesmith.com

_____

_____

_____

11

Credibility multiplies the effectiveness of your sales methodology. In what ways can having greater credibility improve your existing sales process? #SalesCred http://cleesmith.com

---

12

Salespeople can build their credibility with what they say, how they say it, what they do, and what others say about them. #SalesCred http://cleesmith.com

---

13

Salespeople can either increase or decrease their credibility in the actions they take when performing their jobs. What past actions have increased or decreased your credibility? #SalesCred http://cleesmith.com

_____

_____

_____

14

The bigger the sale or the more complex your solution is, the more credible you need to be. #SalesCred http://cleesmith.com

_____

_____

_____

15

The more difficult the economy is, the more important your credibility becomes. Buyers will be seeking every opportunity to reduce risk. Your credibility is the leverage needed to keep from dropping your price. #SalesCred http://cleesmith.com

_____

_____

_____

16

In sales, your level of credibility acts like a magnet. It either attracts your desired buyers to you or it repels your desired buyers away from you. Which way is your magnet turned? #SalesCred http://cleesmith.com

_____

_____

_____

17

How credible are you as a salesperson? More importantly, how credible do your prospects think you are? #SalesCred http://cleesmith.com

_____

_____

_____

THE HIERARCHY OF SALES CREDIBILITY

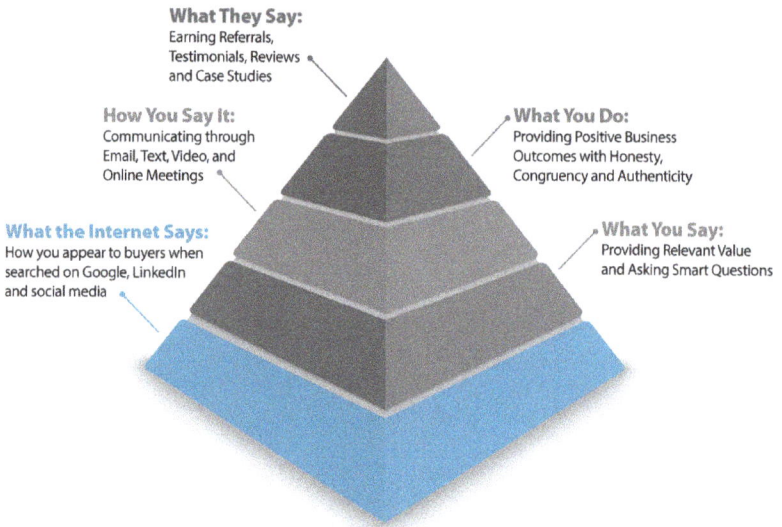

What They Say:
Earning Referrals,
Testimonials, Reviews
and Case Studies

How You Say It:
Communicating through
Email, Text, Video, and
Online Meetings

What the Internet Says:
How you appear to buyers when
searched on Google, LinkedIn
and social media

What You Do:
Providing Positive Business
Outcomes with Honesty,
Congruency and Authenticity

What You Say:
Providing Relevant Value
and Asking Smart Questions

©Copyright 2020 C. Lee Smith - All Rights Reserved

Share the AHA messages from this book socially by going to
https://aha.pub/SalesCred.

*Scan the QR code or use this link to watch the
section videos and more on this section topic:*
https://aha.pub/SalesCresSVs

Section II

What the Internet Says

This section talks about the first area salespeople should focus on, and that's "What the Internet Says."

59% of decision-makers at small-to-midsize companies say they research the salesperson's LinkedIn profile, job history, and social media posts and do a Google search on them before they will meet with the salesperson, according to 2019 SalesFuel research. The larger the customer, the more likely this is to be true.

Your first impression and initial credibility is established by what the buyer finds online—often before you ever know they want to talk to you.

Do you attract buyers with the way you talk and write in your social media accounts? When you post to a blog, write for other sites, put out your own video content, or appear in others' web pages for online interviews, do these activities add value to reinforcing yourself as a credible source of expertise? Salespeople should consistently reinforce their credibility in their online presence.

It is important for sales managers to make sure that the salespeople they're managing are aware of their online presence and what the internet says about them. They should be credible to do business with even before their prospects actually see them face to face.

There are many ways that one can add to and subtract from their credibility with their online presence. This section talks more about that.

By understanding the impact that a salesperson's online presence can have on how they are seen and perceived, sales managers can help them enhance their credibility online.

18

You've heard that "you don't have a second chance to make a first impression." These days, you don't get to make your first impression, Google and LinkedIn does. Does your first impression scream "credible"? #OnlinePresence #SalesCred
https://aha.pub/MitchellLevy

19

Google never forgets and screenshots never forgive.
#OnlinePresence #SalesCred http://cleesmith.com

_____

_____

_____

20

Credibility and Personal Brand are not the same thing.
Personal brand is how you want to be seen. Credibility
is how others actually see you. Aligning both allows
you to make the right first impression. #OnlinePresence
#SalesCred http://cleesmith.com

_____

_____

_____

21

59% of SMB decision makers say they have researched a salesperson online before they met with them. Your #OnlinePresence is "how customers see you before you see them." #SalesCred https://salesfuel.com/selling-to-smbs/ http://cleesmith.com

---

22

How many LinkedIn connections do you have? You come across as credible if hundreds of people find benefit in being connected to you. More importantly, what connections do you have in common with the prospect? #OnlinePresence #SalesCred http://cleesmith.com

---

23

Are your headshots confident, professional and taken sometime in this decade? #OnlinePresence #SalesCred http://cleesmith.com

_____

_____

_____

24

Think about your Ideal Customer Profile (ICP). Does your LinkedIn profile suggest you can solve their problem(s)? How so? If not, what's missing? #OnlinePresence #SalesCred http://cleesmith.com

_____

_____

_____

25

Does your profile make you appear to be a job hopper?
Are buyers wondering if you're worth their time? Will you
be gone in a year? #OnlinePresence #SalesCred
http://cleesmith.com

_____

_____

_____

26

1 out of 7 SMB buyers has blocked a salesperson on
LinkedIn because "they spammed me soon after
connecting with me." #OnlinePresence #SalesCred
https://salesfuel.com/selling-to-smbs/
http://cleesmith.com

_____

_____

_____

27

Spamming a prospect right after connecting with them on LinkedIn gives them the impression that: 1) you don't care about them and 2) you only care about trying to make a sale. #OnlinePresence #SalesCred http://cleesmith.com

---

28

If you have regrettable content online that can't be removed, drown it out with at least 10 other pieces of offsetting content that rebuilds credibility. #OnlinePresence #SalesCred http://cleesmith.com

---

29

If harm was caused by a piece of content that you posted, provide a sincere and proper apology. Then, make several posts that show your enlightened way of thinking. #OnlinePresence #SalesCred http://cleesmith.com

---

30

Write! The most credibility comes from authoring a book. Next is writing an article for a third-party publication or website. Even writing for your own blog can increase your credibility. #OnlinePresence #SalesCred http://cleesmith.com

31

The quality of what you write determines whether your credibility is boosted or harmed — and by how much. #OnlinePresence #SalesCred http://cleesmith.com

---

32

Being quoted in somebody else's writing means the author believes that you are a credible source of expertise. It's also another way that Google will find your name. #OnlinePresence #SalesCred http://cleesmith.com

---

33

You can't fly with the eagles if you run with the turkeys. Your credibility is impacted by whom you associate with. #OnlinePresence #SalesCred http://cleesmith.com

_____

_____

_____

34

Is your outspokenness attracting your ICP or repelling it? While there is some debate among marketers about this, I believe that there are two types of social media: business and personal. #OnlinePresence #SalesCred http://cleesmith.com

_____

_____

_____

35

Take protective measures to lock down personal posts on social media that can be misinterpreted by unknown business prospects — the rules change frequently. With the exception of LinkedIn, avoid using your company's name, website or brand names on your personal profile. #OnlinePresence #SalesCred http://cleesmith.com

---

36

When recording a video, looking away from the camera to read your notes reduces your credibility. #OnlinePresence #SalesCred http://cleesmith.com

---

37

Keep your videos to one minute or less. Rambling decreases your credibility. A concise, meaningful, and memorable video enhances credibility. #OnlinePresence #SalesCred http://cleesmith.com

---

38

One topic, one message, one CTA, and one video. Likes and shares from credible people have a positive impact on your credibility. #OnlinePresence #SalesCred http://cleesmith.com

---

39

When a salesperson's #OnlinePresence screams credibility, they allow people to trust them even before they meet. #SalesCred http://cleesmith.com

_____

_____

_____

40

Think of a prized client you want to win.
What will they find when they search for your name
on Google, LinkedIn and Facebook? #OnlinePresence
#SalesCred http://cleesmith.com

_____

_____

_____

THE HIERARCHY OF SALES CREDIBILITY

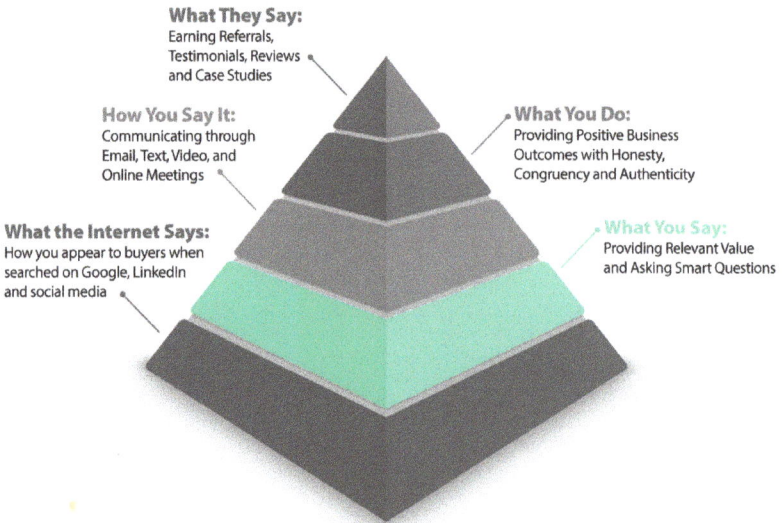

What They Say:
Earning Referrals,
Testimonials, Reviews
and Case Studies

How You Say It:
Communicating through
Email, Text, Video, and
Online Meetings

What You Do:
Providing Positive Business
Outcomes with Honesty,
Congruency and Authenticity

What the Internet Says:
How you appear to buyers when
searched on Google, LinkedIn
and social media

What You Say:
Providing Relevant Value
and Asking Smart Questions

Share the AHA messages from this book socially by going to
https://aha.pub/SalesCred.

*Scan the QR code or use this link to watch the
section videos and more on this section topic:*
https://aha.pub/SalesCresSVs

Section III

What You Say

It's now time to proceed to the next level, which is, "What You Say."

After product knowledge and professionalism, the two things that buyers want most from salespeople are someone who "knows my company/line of business" and someone who "provides relevant ideas to help my business" ("Selling to SMBs" study, SalesFuel, February 2019).

That's why one of the most common questions a salesperson asks that kills credibility is, "Tell me about your business."

Salespeople need to ask the right questions geared toward actually solving the problems of their buyers and not just for the sake of making a sale. The value of what they're selling is dependent on how relevant the products or services are to the buyers, their CEO, and their customers.

Before buyers will trust salespeople with honest answers to these questions, they first need to see if they're credible in providing the solution that is needed to achieve their goals.

During sales calls, salespeople should come in prepared, and genuinely listen to the prospect's questions. That leads to a conversation where salespeople can show their credibility in giving buyers answers to what's important to them and what they actually need, even overcoming objections, if any.

This section explores what salespeople say and how clients actually hear them. Sales managers can use this to guide their salespeople on what to say in order to be seen as credible.

41

What you say can add to or subtract from your credibility. Salespeople need to be wary of the words they use when talking to prospects. They need to use words that project their credibility in order to be heard and respected. #SalesCred http://cleesmith.com

42

Avoid highly suspicious statements like "I'm not trying to sell you anything" (they know your job function), or "if you'll just give me 5 minutes..." (they know you're going to take 30.) Trickery is the tool of a dubious salesperson, not a credible one. #SalesCred http://cleesmith.com

43

Value is not what you say it is or what your marketing
team says it is. It's what the buyer says it is.
@SalesFuel calls this Relevant Value™. If what you say
is not relevant to the buyer, it's not valuable — period.
#SalesCred http://cleesmith.com

44

Relevant Value is not value-add, it's Value x Relevancy. The
most relevant thing is what's most important to the buyer's
CEO — the thing that they talk about in public and in
every internal meeting. #SalesCred http://cleesmith.com

45

In addition to what's most important to the CEO, Relevant Value is also what's important to the buyer, the buyer's boss, and their customers. #SalesCred http://cleesmith.com

_____

_____

_____

46

Address exactly what the buyer or their boss thinks is most important right now. Follow it up with some evidence of proof. Tell a story, and back it up with hard numbers that are believable and verifiable. #SalesCred
http://cleesmith.com

47

Share trade news, industry trends, or primary research from your company. Say, "I saw/read this and thought of you and your current situation." What kind of research and insights do you have available? #SalesCred
http://cleesmith.com

48

Sharing primary and secondary research increases your credibility. It helps you be seen as a credible source of knowledge. #SalesCred http://cleesmith.com

---

49

To be a credible source, use credible sources. The sources of information you cite (or link to) tell the buyer what you think is relevant and accurate. #SalesCred http://cleesmith.com

---

50

The #CPoP (Customer Point of Pain) is the
compass that salespeople use for staying on task
as credible when interacting with prospects.
#SalesCred https://MitchellLevy.com/CPoP

_____

_____

_____

51

Don't be so busy "finding the pain" that you overlook
bigger opportunities. The #CPoP is not just the customer's
point of pain. It can also be an important goal or
aspiration, the customer's point of pleasure. @CLeeSmith
#SalesCred https://MitchellLevy.com/CPoP

_____

_____

_____

52

Discovery is not just a stage, it happens throughout the sales process. In addition to their #CPoP, you must uncover: the consequences for not addressing it, their level of urgency and budget, and how it affects the stakeholders personally. #SalesCred http://cleesmith.com

---

53

Before prospects can trust you with sensitive business information, they first have to see you as having credibility. #SalesCred http://cleesmith.com

---

54

The question that kills a salesperson's credibility the fastest is, "Tell me about your business." How can they think that you can help their business if you don't KNOW their business? #SalesCred http://cleesmith.com

_____

_____

_____

55

Salespeople should avoid asking questions they should already know the answers to.
#SalesCred http://cleesmith.com

_____

_____

_____

56

When you ask smart questions, you look smart. When you ask dumb questions, you don't look like a credible and reliable resource. #SalesCred http://cleesmith.com

_____

_____

_____

57

Although some may think it comes across as humble and authentic, being self-deprecating can be a credibility killer, especially if you make a habit of it. #SalesCred http://cleesmith.com

_____

_____

_____

58

Your product is not the solution. The effective USE of your product to achieve their desired results is the solution. Credible salespeople don't just have product knowledge, they can articulate the Use Case of their product. #SalesCred http://cleesmith.com

_____

_____

_____

59

@Gitomer says, "The person asking the questions is the person leading the conversation." Who's leading your sales dance? #SalesCred http://cleesmith.com

_____

_____

_____

60

The info you learn by asking good questions gives you the leverage you need to build great solutions, overcome objections, and close the sale. If you struggle with any of these, you need to be more curious. #SalesCred http://cleesmith.com

---

61

When salespeople share meaningful information and ask smart questions that enhance their credibility, it makes it much easier for prospects to trust and do business with them. #SalesCred http://cleesmith.com

---

THE HIERARCHY OF SALES CREDIBILITY

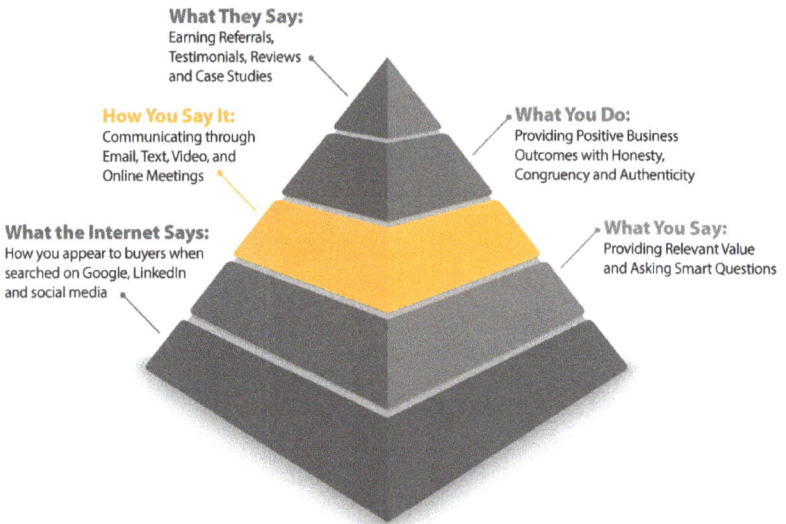

What They Say:
Earning Referrals,
Testimonials, Reviews
and Case Studies

How You Say It:
Communicating through
Email, Text, Video, and
Online Meetings

What You Do:
Providing Positive Business
Outcomes with Honesty,
Congruency and Authenticity

What the Internet Says:
How you appear to buyers when
searched on Google, LinkedIn
and social media

What You Say:
Providing Relevant Value
and Asking Smart Questions

Share the AHA messages from this book socially by going to
https://aha.pub/SalesCred.

Section IV

How You Say It

After knowing "what to say," salespeople then need to focus on "how they say it," both verbally and in writing.

How they communicate is one of the many ways that a salesperson can showcase their credibility or sometimes, their lack thereof.

Do you match the level of professionalism of each client to demonstrate respect for them and their time? Do you show confidence and authority in your choice of words and the way you present yourself in meetings, be it in person or online? Are you supporting or undermining what you say with the way you say it?

To avoid the meaning of words being misconstrued, sales managers should step in and watch how their salespeople are conveying the message to clients, so they are heard the way they want them to be heard, using the tips in this chapter.

Scan the QR code or use this link to watch the section videos and more on this section topic:
https://aha.pub/SalesCresSVs

62

A lack of social awareness may cause salespeople to unintentionally undermine themselves by not noticing how they come across to the buyer -- both in person and online. Can you accurately interpret the emotions of people with whom you interact? #SalesCred
http://cleesmith.com

_____

_____

_____

63

Since COVID-19, salespeople are sending more emails than ever. The #1 goal of a sales email is to get a response. Before that can happen, it must: get through the spam filters, get opened, and get read. #SalesCred http://cleesmith.com

_____

_____

_____

64

Marketing email is one message written for many people. Sales email is one message written for one person. Do you know what the difference should be when writing them? #SalesCred http://cleesmith.com

_____

_____

_____

65

Not matching the level of professionalism of the recipient may cause misunderstandings with how you conduct business. Don't be too casual, use slang, or assume a level of friendship that doesn't exist. #SalesCred http://cleesmith.com

_____

_____

_____

66

The more important an email or text is, the more effort you need to make to proofread and revise it. A typo or punctuation mistake is not harmful to credibility, but poor grammar is. #SalesCred http://cleesmith.com

_____

_____

_____

67

When writing emails, make it obvious that a real person wrote it. If it reads and feels like a template, you'll be perceived as someone who doesn't care enough about the person you're sending it to. #SalesCred http://cleesmith.com

_____

_____

_____

68

Always avoid using spammy words in email.
They'll never read your email if they never see it.
#SalesCred https://aha.pub/SpammyWords

_____

_____

_____

69

Being brief in email can increase your credibility. 50-125
words, tops, is good; 75-100 words is the sweet spot.
#SalesCred http://cleesmith.com

_____

_____

_____

70

As a salesperson, including relevant certifications/ badges in your email signature increases your credibility. #SalesCred http://cleesmith.com

71

Never have a complex conversation by email. If your email contains two meaty paragraphs, it's better to scrap it and pick up the phone. #SalesCred http://cleesmith.com

72

Be responsive! One business day maximum. Salespeople often say they'll be there for their clients if they have problems or questions. Credibility comes from walking the talk. #SalesCred http://cleesmith.com

_____

_____

_____

73

It's better to say that you don't know the answer to their question, but you'll find it for them, than to try to BS your way through. Acting like a know-it-all damages your credibility. #SalesCred http://cleesmith.com

_____

_____

_____

74

In sales, you're either making money or making excuses. Blaming the traffic, the weather, your computer, your boss, or a co-worker for your failure to deliver is not the action of a credible salesperson.
#SalesCred http://cleesmith.com

_____

_____

_____

75

As a salesperson, avoid using qualifiers in your wording (such as: maybe, probably, likely, possibly, somewhat). Using them subtracts credibility.
#SalesCred http://cleesmith.com

_____

_____

_____

76

As a salesperson, making assumptions that turn out not to be true is a credkiller. Ask clarifying questions. #SalesCred http://cleesmith.com

_____

_____

_____

77

Avoid ambiguity whenever possible. There is comfort to the buyer in knowing EXACTLY what you plan to do for them, how much it will cost, and how/when it will be delivered. It also reduces the chances of misunderstanding and disappointment later. #SalesCred http://cleesmith.com

_____

_____

78

Starting a sentence with "My clients have told me that.../We're seeing.../We're hearing.../One question I get asked about _____ is..." builds credibility if what follows is accurate and insightful. #SalesCred http://cleesmith.com

79

Want to be seen as an authority? Use authoritative language. Be careful not to be bossy or condescending. Use active voice ("Our company hired three new people") instead of passive voice ("Three people were hired by our company"). #SalesCred http://cleesmith.com

80

How you say it also means knowing when to shut up. Salespeople who don't show a genuine interest in what the prospect has to say are less likable and thus, less credible. #SalesCred http://cleesmith.com

_____

_____

_____

81

Not showing up prepared for a meeting shows a lack of respect for the prospect and their time. So does showing up late. Think, "early is on time and on time is late." #SalesCred http://cleesmith.com

_____

_____

_____

82

When coming to a meeting, do you research who is going to be in it? If not, don't come at all. #SalesCred
http://cleesmith.com

83

"Your visual appearance influences the way people judge you," Sylvie di Giusto said on the "Manage Smarter" podcast. Does your appearance make the buyer feel comfortable working with you?
https://managesmarter.com #SalesCred

84

Practicing your delivery is important, but avoid coming across as "too slick." Being the overly-extroverted, silver-tongued salesperson raises the buyer's defenses. Introverts actually have the power to disarm the buyer. #SalesCred http://cleesmith.com

_____

_____

_____

85

When interacting with someone, be human and show empathy. Understanding their situation from their unique point of view adds to your credibility as a salesperson. #SalesCred http://cleesmith.com

---

86

Being in the front of the room (presenting, on a panel) increases your credibility. #SalesCred http://cleesmith.com

---

87

Being mentioned by name by the leader of the meeting (if it's not you) builds your credibility. #SalesCred #Credust http://cleesmith.com

_____

_____

_____

88

When presenting, reading your notes or your slides hurts your credibility. #SalesCred http://cleesmith.com

_____

_____

_____

89

Mispronouncing or misspelling the names of commonly-known people or industry terms gives away credibility. #Credcrud #SalesCred https://credcrud.com

_____

_____

_____

90

As a salesperson, your body language speaks a thousand words. What does your body say when you're in front other people? #SalesCred http://cleesmith.com

_____

_____

_____

91

Stepping back from others, turning your back to them, and not making eye contact are three ways that you give away credibility when speaking in meetings. #SalesCred http://cleesmith.com

_____

_____

_____

92

As a salesperson, you need to match the level of mood of others in the meeting — don't be too stiff or too casual. #SalesCred http://cleesmith.com

---

93

Trying to make a sale virtually? Don't fumble with audio/video settings. Use the microphone-check and speaker-check features before joining the meeting. Make sure the buyer has the impression that you've done this before. #SalesCred http://cleesmith.com

---

94

Video backgrounds should be clean and non-distracting. Books on your area of expertise build credibility and so do awards you have won or certificates you've earned. When all else fails, use a virtual background. #SalesCred http://cleesmith.com

---

95

Credible salespeople are the ones who know when to shut up and listen to the buyer instead of cueing up the next brilliant sales point they want to make. The most useful info they share is usually at the end. #SalesCred
http://cleesmith.com

_____

_____

_____

96

When you speak and deliver words credibly in every situation, you allow yourself to be perceived as someone to do business with. #SalesCred
http://cleesmith.com

_____

_____

_____

THE HIERARCHY OF SALES CREDIBILITY

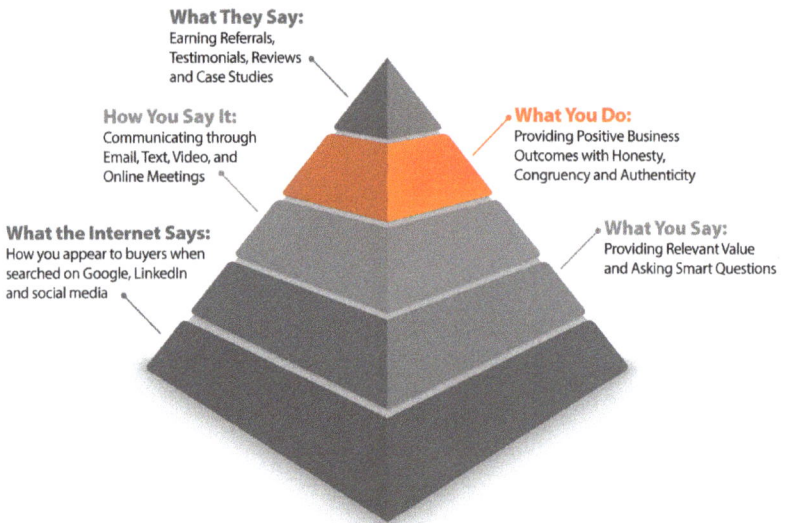

What They Say:
Earning Referrals,
Testimonials, Reviews
and Case Studies

How You Say It:
Communicating through
Email, Text, Video, and
Online Meetings

What You Do:
Providing Positive Business
Outcomes with Honesty,
Congruency and Authenticity

What the Internet Says:
How you appear to buyers when
searched on Google, LinkedIn
and social media

What You Say:
Providing Relevant Value
and Asking Smart Questions

Share the AHA messages from this book socially by going to
https://aha.pub/SalesCred.

*Scan the QR code or use this link to watch the
section videos and more on this section topic:*
https://aha.pub/SalesCresSVs

Section V

What You Do

After learning about the areas where "words" are dominant, it's now time to focus on action.

"What you do" as a salesperson needs to support what you say. When words are backed up by actions, credibility is demonstrated.

The key to building credibility through "what you do" centers around honesty, congruency, and authenticity.

The best way to build credibility (and build future sales) is to produce positive business outcomes. Is what you're doing focused on the most pressing end goal as spelled out by the prospective client? Credible salespeople don't have to offer anything outrageous to the point of misleading their clients. This is a desperate move that does not demonstrate credibility.

Can you connect the dots and collaborate to build a proposal that will achieve the result the buyers seek? Do you avoid selling the "product of the month" or selling them more than they need? After the contract is signed, do you follow up to make sure you've delivered what you've promised?

This section covers how important salespeople's actions are in consistently and effectively building credibility. A good understanding of the importance of always delivering what's promised will allow sales managers to help their salespeople build credibility and build future sales.

97

A salesperson's actions should be geared
toward helping clients achieve their goals.
When they are, not only will they produce positive
business outcomes, but they will also gain credibility.
#SalesCred http://cleesmith.com

_____

_____

_____

98

Do you want to know who you are? Don't ask. Act!
Action will delineate and define you.—Thomas Jefferson
via http://cleesmith.com #SalesCred

99

Show up when you show up! Are you there mentally,
not just physically? Did you come early,
arrive prepared, and show your heart?
#SalesCred https://aha.pub/MitchellLevy

100

Outcome leads to income. The best way to build your credibility and get repeat sales is to produce positive business outcomes. @cleesmith #SalesCred http://cleesmith.com

_____

_____

_____

101

Your clients don't care about YOUR sales, they care about THEIR sales. Focus all your activity on them, not on you. #SalesCred http://cleesmith.com

---

102

Never say you're offering clients something special because you have to meet quota or you're trying to win a sales contest. A credible professional doesn't have to do this, a desperate one does. #SalesCred http://cleesmith.com

---

103

Credible salespeople don't half-ass things. They bust their entire ass doing a few things well, rather than taking on too much and letting the quality of their work slip. #SalesCred @cleesmith @salesfuel

---

104

Never take advantage of a buyer. If the names on the proposal were reversed and you were the buyer, does it still look like a good business deal? If not, don't expect them to buy from you again. #SalesCred http://cleesmith.com

---

105

Credibility is built when you propose solutions
that are in the best interests of all parties involved.
Credibility is destroyed when you only think of yourself.
#SalesCred http://cleesmith.com

106

The key to building credibility through "what you do"
centers around honesty, congruency, and authenticity.
In other words, sell to others like you would sell to your
mom. #SalesCred http://cleesmith.com

107

#SalesCred requires follow-through and accountability. Always deliver what you promised and admit your obvious mistakes. http://cleesmith.com

_____

_____

_____

108

If others are involved in the delivery of your solution, double-check to make sure they're on point and on schedule. #SalesCred http://cleesmith.com

_____

_____

_____

109

"Under promise, over deliver," says @Tom_Peters. Whenever you have the opportunity to meaningfully go above and beyond to delight a client, do it! It is one of the most sure-fire ways that What You Do will build your credibility. #SalesCred http://cleesmith.com

---

110

There is no such thing as a credible hypocrite. #SalesCred requires congruence. What you say and what you do must always be in alignment. http://cleesmith.com

---

111

Think of an account that you've tried to save recently. What actions (or lack thereof) put you in that position? #SalesCred http://cleesmith.com

---

112

Credible people do business with credible people. They know what high performance, high service levels, and high accountability looks like. Make sure you do too. #SalesCred http://cleesmith.com

---

113

Credibility is lost when expectations aren't met. Credibility is won when expectations are exceeded. -- @cleesmith #SalesCred http://cleesmith.com

---

114

Credibility is fragile. It takes many actions over time to effectively build credibility with a buyer, but only one time being caught in a lie to lose it. Handle with care! #SalesCred http://cleesmith.com

---

THE HIERARCHY OF SALES CREDIBILITY

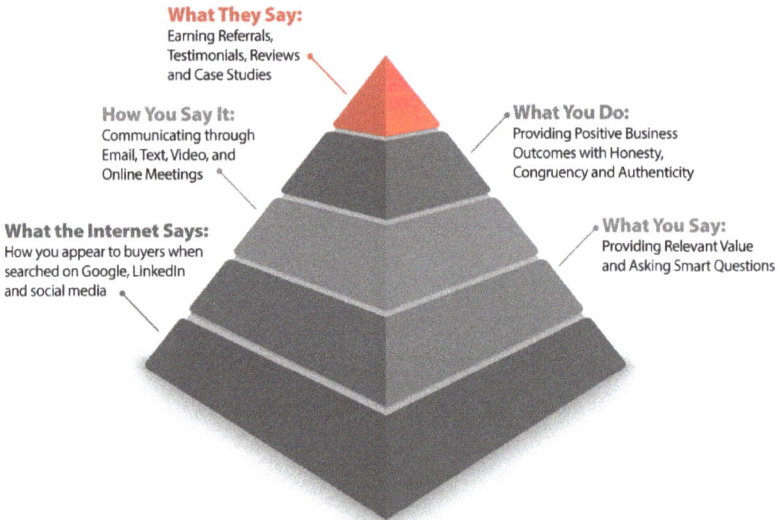

What They Say:
Earning Referrals,
Testimonials, Reviews
and Case Studies

How You Say It:
Communicating through
Email, Text, Video, and
Online Meetings

What You Do:
Providing Positive Business
Outcomes with Honesty,
Congruency and Authenticity

What the Internet Says:
How you appear to buyers when
searched on Google, LinkedIn
and social media

What You Say:
Providing Relevant Value
and Asking Smart Questions

Share the AHA messages from this book socially by going to
https://aha.pub/SalesCred.

*Scan the QR code or use this link to watch the
section videos and more on this section topic:*
https://aha.pub/SalesCresSVs

Section VI

What They Say

Now, it's time to talk about the pinnacle of sales credibility, which is, "What they say."

28% of North American decision-makers say that "a testimonial from a satisfied customer can influence my buying decision if it seems credible" ("Selling to SMBs" study, SalesFuel, February 2019). Even more will share a good experience with their friends by posting a positive review on social media.

What matters most at the end of the day is what customers say about you, your company, and your products. Most salespeople have big egos, too much bravado and do a lot of bragging without a lot of proof. You stand out from the pack by having others do the talking for you in the form of referrals, testimonials, introductions, positive reviews, and success stories.

When you show that you are empathetic to others' needs more than your own, buyers are much more willing to introduce you to their friends and colleagues so you can help them solve problems and achieve their goals. This is when you know that your credibility has been converted into trust.

An important role of sales managers is to teach salespeople how to be a super-connector, which is a great way to get referrals. Reciprocity can easily happen in the sales industry when someone makes someone else credible, increasing their stature, sharing their expertise, and vice versa.

This section tackles the benefits of having a continuing professional relationship between the salespeople they're managing and their clients through referrals, testimonials, and introductions. Sales managers can show their salespeople how these endorsements can strongly build their credibility throughout the sales process.

115

Beyond the sales numbers, it's what your customers say about you — and their experience with you — that matters most. Do they say that you're INcredible or UNcredible? #SalesCred http://cleesmith.com

---

116

Referrals, testimonials, and introductions are how one person shares their credust with you (see https://credust.com). @HappyAbout #SalesCred

---

117

What speaks more to somebody who doesn't know
your record — you talking yourself up or somebody they
know/respect talking you up? #SalesCred
http://cleesmith.com

118

If you say it, it's bragging. If they say it, it's proof.
@Gitomer via http://cleesmith.com
#Testimonials #SalesCred

119

Be a super-connector — you can get #Referrals by giving them first. Of course, the referrals you give need to be credible. #SalesCred http://cleesmith.com

_____

_____

_____

120

Ask for an introduction from the buyer to their boss or another prospect. Whatever their credibility is will be shared with you. #SalesCred http://cleesmith.com

_____

_____

_____

121

Ask, "Can I tell them that you suggested I contact them?" or "Can I tell them that I'm working with you?" #Introduction #SalesCred http://cleesmith.com

_____

_____

_____

122

Give LinkedIn endorsements to the buyer first to get them in return. How many endorsements have you given this month? #SalesCred http://cleesmith.com

_____

_____

_____

123

Giving undeserved #Recommendations hurts your credibility. #SalesCred http://cleesmith.com

_____

_____

_____

124

28% of SMB decision makers say that "a testimonial from a satisfied customer can influence my buying decision if it seems credible." #SalesCred https://salesfuel.com/selling-to-smbs/ http://cleesmith.com

---

125

Referrals, testimonials, and introductions build credibility throughout the sales process (i.e., in prospecting, when connecting with the decision maker, as part of your proposal, when overcoming objections and closing). #SalesCred http://cleesmith.com

---

126

Reciprocity can easily happen in sales when someone makes someone else credible. This can increase their stature and share their expertise in the most credible way possible. #Credust #SalesCred
https://aha.pub/MitchellLevy

_____

_____

_____

127

Introduce your customer to other people that can help their business. It will help them achieve their goals and also let them see you as a business partner, increasing your credibility. #SalesCred http://cleesmith.com

_____

_____

_____

128

When reaching out to a client to ask for a testimonial, never encourage them to be anything but completely honest about their experience with you and what you sell. #SalesCred http://cleesmith.com

---

129

Exaggeration kills credibility, whether it's you saying it or someone saying it about you. Unbelievable or untruthful testimonials do not come across as authentic or credible. #SalesCred http://cleesmith.com

---

130

A recent eConsultancy survey found that 61% of customers read online reviews before making a purchase decision. Using reviews on your site could result in an 18% sales boost! #SalesCred
https://aha.pub/eConsultancySurvey
http://cleesmith.com

_____

_____

_____

131

The more others can hear from clients you've delighted, the likelier your chances to generate more high-quality leads. That's because your clients have already qualified you for future buyers. #SalesCred http://cleesmith.com

_____

_____

_____

132

You don't just have one Hierarchy of Sales Credibility. You have a pyramid for each and every lead you call on. You become a truly credible salesperson when you can turn multiple prospects into accounts that reach the top level - and will sing your praises to others. #SalesCred

_____

_____

_____

THE HIERARCHY OF SALES CREDIBILITY

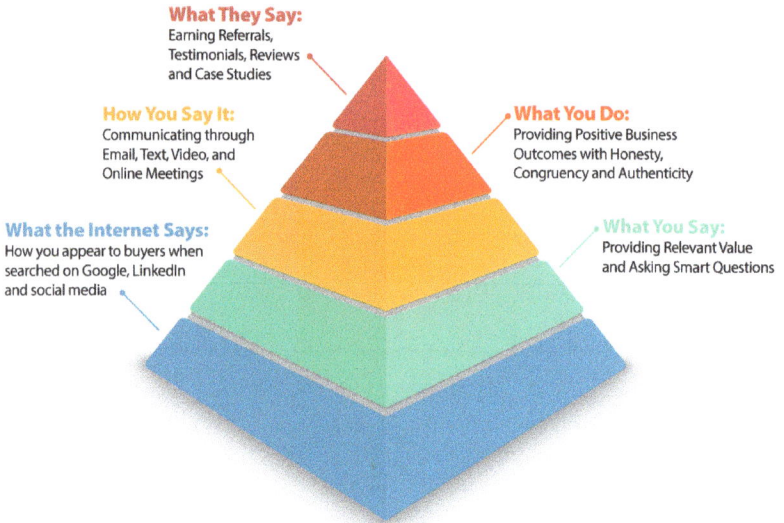

What They Say:
Earning Referrals,
Testimonials, Reviews
and Case Studies

How You Say It:
Communicating through
Email, Text, Video, and
Online Meetings

What You Do:
Providing Positive Business
Outcomes with Honesty,
Congruency and Authenticity

What the Internet Says:
How you appear to buyers when
searched on Google, LinkedIn
and social media

What You Say:
Providing Relevant Value
and Asking Smart Questions

Share the AHA messages from this book socially by going to
https://aha.pub/SalesCred.

Section VII

Conclusion

Sales credibility is an all-encompassing quality that salespeople need to have in abundance. Unfortunately, not everybody consciously takes this to heart. But consider this an opportunity for you!

Nowadays, the world is seeing not only a credibility deficit but also a credibility crisis. With the notable exception of politics, this is nowhere more evident than in sales. The good news is, having a high degree of credibility enables you to stand apart from your competition, gaining you access to information and top-level decision-makers that the others won't have.

To be truly successful in building and maintaining credibility, salespeople should always be mindful of:

1. what the internet says,
2. what they say,
3. how they say it,
4. what they do, and
5. what customers say about them

These five levels essentially reveal a salesperson's philosophy and character. If you approach each level with integrity and hard work, especially in the heat of the sale when others may be taking shortcuts, you will be seen as credible.

But keep in mind that credibility must be maintained after it is built with consistent and reliable efforts every day. It takes a true commitment toward being known, being likable, and being trustworthy in all you say and do.

When salespeople have credibility and continually strive to be credible, they are citizens of Credibility Nation™. In Credibility Nation, salespeople are all about having empathy, being educated, and staying curious, showing you care, and having honesty, congruency, and authenticity. Here, salespeople have high business acumen while still being good humans, not robots merely meeting quotas.

With this book, sales managers can effectively help their salespeople decide where they are going to plant their flag and guide them to choose the right path. Are they going to be non-credible, untrustworthy, and part of the Dubious Nation™? Or are they going to help others achieve their goals, producing positive business outcomes, and become citizens in Credibility Nation?

Scan the QR code or use this link to watch the section videos and more on this section topic:
https://aha.pub/SalesCresSVs

133

Sales credibility is an all-encompassing quality that salespeople need to pay great attention to. It is how buyers qualify YOU. Without it, building your sales pipeline is much harder. http://cleesmith.com

_____

_____

_____

134

Think of building #SalesCred as a pyramid,
the pinnacle of which is receiving referrals and
testimonials that make your future sales much easier.
http://cleesmith.com

_____

_____

_____

135

What the internet says about you, what you say,
how you say it, what you do, and what your customers
say all reveal your philosophy and character — and
whether you're credible enough to do business with.
#SalesCred http://cleesmith.com

136

Credible salespeople have high levels of business
acumen, humanity, and empathy for others. It's the value
we bring to today's marketplace that separates us from
robots and computers. #SalesCred http://cleesmith.com

137

There's a fine line between confidence and arrogance. One can be very credible. The other is eventually found out to be not credible. Stay humble and authentic. #SalesCred http://cleesmith.com

_____

_____

_____

138

Salespeople who are coachable, are open to what their mentors and managers share with them, invest more time in learning, and have great attitudes are the ones who stay on top of their game. #SalesCred http://cleesmith.com

_____

_____

_____

139

Your credibility is worth much more than any sale. Never compromise your principles, even if a competitor is doing it. You'll feel great about the deals you've won, and you'll win friends, which leads to even more sales. #SalesCred http://cleesmith.com

---

140

Good sales managers improve numbers. Great sales managers improve PEOPLE. Start by helping your team members improve their credibility. https://salescred.com

---

140+1

You may have noticed a common thread through the 140 CredTips we've presented here: intelligence.

Whether it be pre-call research, business acumen, emotional intelligence, or sales know-how, being a lifelong learner gives you the edge in building and maintaining credibility.

Some sales veterans—even the successful ones—may find it tempting "go with their gut" and say, "I've been doing this for 20 years, so I know all about…" But the world is not the same as it was 20 days ago, much less 20 years ago, and neither is sales.

Knowledge that comes from learning from credible sources—and applying that knowledge—is a vital part of what it takes to be seen as a credible salesperson who can provide Relevant Value to customers, enable buyers to solve problems, and help them achieve their goals.

Salespeople who are coachable, are open to what their mentors and managers share with them, invest more time in learning, and have positive, optimistic attitudes are the ones who can elevate their game when the marketplace is sluggish.

Always be learning.
Always be helpful.
Always be credible.
Always, in all ways.

Bonus Section. The 7 C's of Pre-Call Intelligence for Highly Credible Salespeople

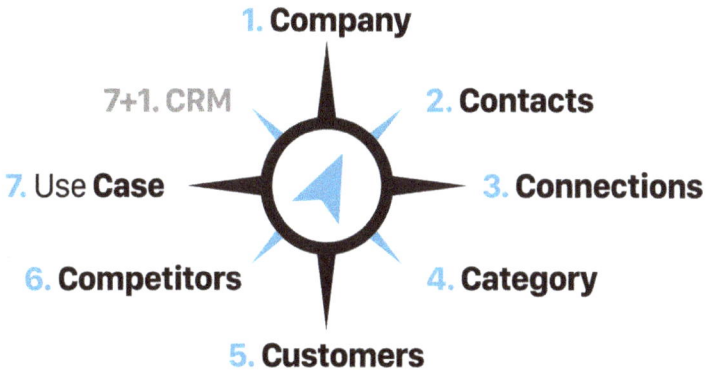

THE 7 C'S OF PRE-CALL INTELLIGENCE
for Highly Credible Salespeople

1. **Company**

7+1. CRM

2. **Contacts**

7. Use **Case**

3. **Connections**

6. **Competitors**

4. **Category**

5. **Customers**

In this book, I wrote about how a buyer uses credibility to qualify (or disqualify) a seller. Credibility is the very thing that determines whether a buyer replies to your email, agrees to take a meeting, or decides they want to do business with you.

Nowhere is credibility more evident to a buyer than the amount of effort the salesperson puts into pre-call intelligence. Salespeople who take a moment beforehand to find something of relevance to the buyer that they can share, instead of just winging it and trying to get by on personality, are perceived as more credible. They're also more helpful and have a far greater chance of connecting the dots for the buyer.

The COVID-19 pandemic has taught all of us that it's possible for many businesses to operate entirely online. The prospects you're targeting have realized they don't need to meet with salespeople in person to purchase products and services. In addition to those challenges, buyers now take the time to learn about you, the salesperson, online before they meet with you. They're checking your LinkedIn profile, your social media, and even doing a Google search on you.

At a minimum, shouldn't you be doing that as well? Yet, nearly half of salespeople don't even bother to check a prospect's website. Consider that to be a big opportunity for you!

When you commit to practicing the 7 C's of pre-call intelligence for sales credibility, you're also committing to learning as much as you can so that you understand how your product(s) can positively impact a buyer's business.

If your role is to prospect for new business, it's your job to study your buyer, their company, and their business category. If your role is to support an existing account, you should know what's changed since the last time you made contact.

Additionally, by keeping your information current and maintaining your image as a polished and go-to sales professional, you're also increasing your credibility.

1. Company

1. COMPANY

Once you've identified the company you want to sell to, it's time to narrow your research funnel. You need several key pieces of information in order to build your file on the target company.

Revenue

One of the most difficult pieces of information to obtain about any private company is their total revenue. Small private companies like to protect that information, especially from their competitors. If your review of local media reports on the company turns up nothing, you can guesstimate their revenue. SalesFuel, for example, provides its clients with estimates of sales per employee by category and by market in the U.S.

Tip: A good rule of thumb is to use $180,000 times the number of full-time employees on a company payroll. So, if your prospect has 10 employees, their revenue is roughly $1.8 million.

For larger organizations, check out online resources. Publicly traded companies report their revenue on their 10-K reports. Those reports also give you access to important trends. You can tell whether a company's revenue and profit is growing or shrinking. At the end of their fiscal year, companies file 10-K reports with the government and usually issue press releases. You'll find those releases on their websites.

History and Mission

Reviewing the company history gives you great insight into where they've been and where they're going. Imagine mentioning in a meeting that you know the company started out as a country store 150 years ago. Then, you ask how they are celebrating such a milestone anniversary. The people you're talking with will know you've done your homework and your credibility will jump. The same holds true for the company's mission. When you understand the mission that the company has committed to, you will understand the motivation of its key leaders.

While the history page on the company website is a great resource, the results of a Google search will turn up more intelligence. Scroll several pages of search findings to determine whether the company or any of its top employees are involved in litigation. Also, consider searching a site like Glassdoor, which will give you insight into what employees think about an organization. Keep in mind, though, that Glassdoor does not appear to verify the employment of "employees" who post reviews about their past employers.

Funding and Ownership

Some of the companies you'll target will have been bootstrapped by the owner and founder. Those smaller private companies often grow slowly unless they decide to seek outside investment. You'll find hints about how a company is funded on the About Us page.

News releases and listings on proprietary sites like G2 Crowd will reveal whether the company has accepted outside investment, such as from a venture fund or another organization that may eventually try to purchase them.

Tip: If an organization has taken venture money, the leaders will be under increasing pressure to scale and show a return on investment. At least one of the decision-makers you'll be talking with may be a plant by the venture fund in order to ensure the company is on the right track. If you impress that individual with your credibility, you could open the door to sales made with other companies in the venture fund's portfolio.

In a venture-funded company, cash infusions take place over the course of several years. If that's the case with your target company, learn what round of venture funding they're in. After the mezzanine round, they'll be ready to go public, and that's often a time when an organization has plenty of money to spend.

You may also sell to a nonprofit organization such as a local government entity. Because taxpayer money is being used to buy products and services, the decision-making process can be much slower in those organizations. They often follow a complex set of rules to ensure no bias exists in the purchase process.

Technographics
As the speed of commerce continues to increase, so does the need to operate more efficiently. Companies continually invest in new technology as a way to stay one step ahead of the competition. Your prospect might be willing to change one of their technology platforms for a guaranteed return on their investment. In order to speak intelligently about the cost savings your prospect might achieve with your solution, you should have a complete outline of the technology they're currently using. In some organizations, the existing technology may be underutilized because employees don't like the interface or some other aspect of the product. That dissatisfaction could be a way into the organization for you.

Your firmographics research should reveal the size of your prospect company, its number of locations, and its funding and ownership profile. In addition, you should determine whether they're profitable. If they're not, find out how long it's been since they were profitable. That review can lead you to understand whether they are in a financial situation to invest in your solution. That analysis can also help you analyze whether the firm, if it's an international conglomerate, is likely to buy from a seller who has previously only worked with local SMBs.

Product Lines
While you know which industry your prospect operates in, remember that most companies sell more than one product or service. Check out your prospect's website and conduct an online search to learn what they sell. You should know if they recently discontinued a product or if they launched a new brand. It's not always easy to figure out the percentage of revenue each product and service line adds to company revenue but keep digging into the details to find out.

Sales professionals who devote extra time to researching the buyer's company make the right impression and build credibility. Nearly 44% of buyers in our SMB Purchase Survey said they select a salesperson who knows their company and their line of business. Unfortunately, according to the Voice of the Sales Rep study, only 52% of U.S. sales reps check out a prospect's website as part of their pre-call preparation.

Momentum

Understanding a company's momentum is an excellent way to estimate how quickly they respond to change and how quickly they try to initiate change in the marketplace. Organizations that rarely release new products or services could be ranked as low momentum. You may have better luck going after companies with higher momentum, i.e., those that are actively changing and making decisions.

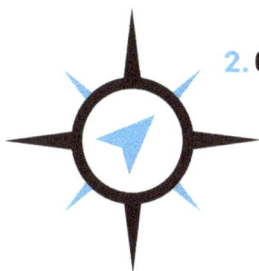

1. Company

2. **Contacts**

2. CONTACTS

Now that you understand the company you're targeting, it's time to increase your credibility by improving your visibility. Business leaders spend plenty of time and energy shielding themselves from the relentless outreach of sales professionals. If you cast yourself as just another sales professional, you'll never get past the gatekeeper.

The best approach is to position yourself as a sales professional who business leaders want to connect with. How does that work? Start by understanding whose attention and approval you need. There are three categories of professionals in an organization to target.

Primary decision-makers – Those company leaders will sign the paperwork for the solution you're selling. They sweat over details like the budget. If they opt to go with the wrong seller, it's their reputations and possibly their jobs that are on the line.

Primary influencers – Those people are likely to attend your presentations and talk behind the scenes with decision-makers. Influencers may have subject-matter expertise. For example, if your solution contains technology, an influencer will have an opinion on whether that technology will be difficult to incorporate into the buyer's legacy systems.

Tip: Primary influencers can also be leaders-in-training. Make sure you understand their motivations. In some cases, they'll try to impress the primary decision-makers with their knowledge and ability to think independently. In other cases, they'll simply go along with what they think the decision-makers are thinking.

Stakeholders – Those individuals hold the jobs that will be most significantly impacted by the solution you're selling. If they sense you're selling a threat to their future employment, don't expect them to be friendly. On the other hand, these employees can be your biggest supporters when they believe you can make their jobs easier.

Check out the corporate website bio for each person on your list. LinkedIn will be your top go-to site when you're building your knowledge base in your CRM. Other social sites, like Facebook, can also round out the information you need.

At a minimum, your profile for each of your contacts should include:

- ❑ Name
- ❑ Current position in the company
- ❑ Length of time in the current position
- ❑ Length of time with the company
- ❑ Previous position in the company
- ❑ Previous employers
- ❑ Length of time in the industry
- ❑ Professional areas of expertise
- ❑ Industry and company awards
- ❑ Certifications

For next-level credibility with existing accounts, your profile should also include:

- ❑ Birthdays
- ❑ Personal interests and leisure activities
- ❑ Family members
- ❑ Pets

- ❑ Educational background
- ❑ Causes or nonprofit organizations that are important to them
- ❑ Their favorite things (restaurants, places to shop, sports teams, vacation spots, beverages, snacks, etc.)

That is where pre-call intelligence stops for many sales reps. For highly credible salespeople, the third C is where you start connecting the dots.

1. Company

2. Contacts

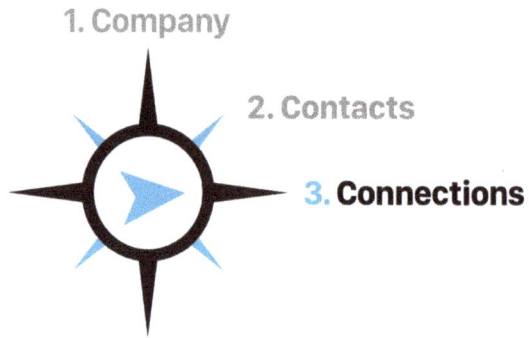

3. **Connections**

3. CONNECTIONS

Connections can be your credibility currency. You can enhance your credibility by making connections with a buyer outside of the specific selling situation you're in. The more connections you have, the more your reputation grows. People become familiar with your name. They begin to think of you as a professional with expertise in your specific field. Sellers with a proven track record will find more doors open to them. Even the toughest gatekeepers are more willing to let a well-known and well-regarded seller into the office.

Work, but don't force, those connections on multiple levels. Mine them on a past, present, and future continuum.

The Past

Online research will reveal if you and a buyer went to the same school. Find out if you both worked for the same organization in the past. If you worked for a company at different time periods, you may be able to ask, "Whom do I know that you know?" Coming up with a common name and agreeing on that individual's great strengths can be an icebreaker and a credibility builder.

Don't forget about volunteer efforts. You may have both volunteered or supported a charitable organization. Discussing the latest event that the charity held and the impact of the charity's work in the community builds your credibility as a generous and empathetic individual.

The Present

To connect with what's happening in your prospect's personal life, expand your online search. Sharing an interest in the same sport builds credibility quickly. Kiteboarding, anyone? Remember to stay humble and be self-deprecating if you've won awards. Nobody appreciates a braggart, especially someone you're selling to.

Another common and emotional connection centers on children. If you and your buyer are both enduring early morning swim team practices, long track meets on weekends, or teaching teens how to drive, you can credibly show empathy for the buyer's personal situation. The buyer who senses that you are empathetic on a personal level will be inclined to trust you in a business deal.

The Future

You can lay the groundwork for strengthening future connections by asking questions on a site like LinkedIn. When your prospect answers these questions, you can begin to build a long-term relationship. Part of that process includes giving testimonials. If your prospect answers one of your questions, thanking them and touting their expertise on LinkedIn will attract their attention. The more testimonials you give, as long as they are valid, the more positive reinforcement you can expect in return. Prospects who see testimonials on your social sites will grant you higher credibility.

The world of connections extends beyond you and a prospect. Check your resources to determine whether anyone in your company knows a prospect. A thorough online search will also reveal whether your prospect has a connection with any of your current clients. And don't forget to check out your other prospects to find possible connections.

You'll also want to target specific individuals as you build credibility. Engage in influencer networking. For example, the key contacts in your buyer's organization may hesitate to decide until an industry thought leader has favorably reviewed your product or service. Getting a key influencer to speak about your credibility and the credibility of the product or service you're selling can open many doors.

Tip: Part of your job in sales is to be a super connector, especially if you're in business development. The more people you know and can reliably connect to others, the more the buzz will increase about you. Higher buzz translates to increased credibility.

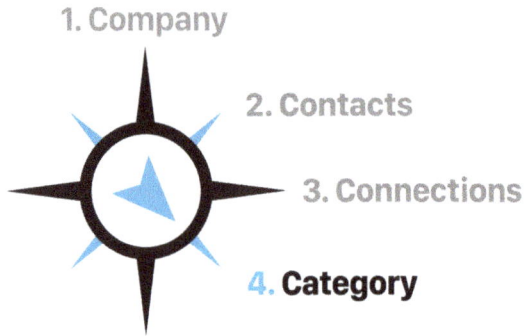

1. Company

2. Contacts

3. Connections

4. Category

4. CATEGORY

In the eyes of most buyers, a salesperson can't help their business if they don't KNOW their business. That is why staying on top of the business category or industry for each prospect is so important.

When you begin your journey as a sales professional with a new organization, your manager typically assigns you a business category or sector to develop. Every business category has an addressable market. Every business in the category is competing for a part of that market.

In some categories, the market grows only as quickly as the population does. The grocery industry is a good example of a mature slow-growing category. On the other hand, a business category that is young in its life cycle, such as cloud computing, has a quickly expanding market. Keep in mind that some categories do well when the economy is expanding. Other categories, such as discount stores, for example, do better when the economy is contracting.

The companies in every category compete by continuously developing new products and services.

They're also encountering opportunities and challenges as the market changes. Some categories face disintermediation. Companies competing in that type of market will see their revenue streams decrease and eventually disappear—think video stores—unless they change their business models.

While it's important to know how you stack up against other solution providers in a category, keep your focus on your prospect. How can you make sense of what's happening in the prospect's category? Start by reading business journals, industry trade journals, and analyst projections.

Tip: Companies that are planning to go public file an S-1 report with the Securities and Exchange Commission (SEC). These S-1 reports often contain an industry overview and outlook section. Why? Because the S-1 report is designed to show potential investors details about the addressable market for the category.

To be an expert in your category, you should know the names of the companies with the largest market share. Stay current on mergers and acquisitions in the industry. Any change in ownership means changes in top personnel and the decision-makers you want to reach.

Good category knowledge will help you develop your best conversation starters and discovery questions. At the very least, you should know the following information about your category. This will allow you to determine where your target company stands relative to the category averages.

- ❑ Financial benchmarks
- ❑ Peak sales seasons
- ❑ Top merchandise / service lines by revenue
- ❑ Average client retention rate (for B2B accounts)
- ❑ Typical advertising / marketing / promotional efforts
- ❑ Social media metrics
- ❑ Most popular SEO keywords
- ❑ Sales trends
- ❑ Challenges threatening category growth
- ❑ Emerging opportunities for category growth

Ultimately, your category research will help you in three ways:

- You'll determine which companies to target.
- You'll develop a broad and current knowledge base which builds your credibility.
- You'll be able to use category trends to ask intelligent discovery questions of your prospects/accounts during every sales call. If they aren't aware of a new development you're asking about, you're providing value and thus, increasing your credibility.

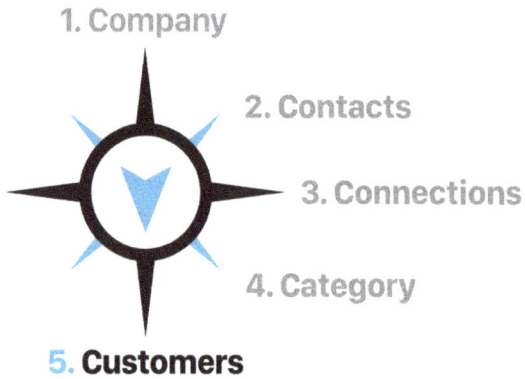

1. Company

2. Contacts

3. Connections

4. Category

5. **Customers**

5. CUSTOMERS

Some salespeople research their top prospects just long enough to know about their core customers. That is a good start. But to be perceived as a highly credible salesperson, you don't just need to know about YOUR customers. You need to understand THEIR customers.

At a top level, you should know whether your prospect targets consumers (B2C), businesses (B2B), or a mix of customers (hybrid). Check out who they want to have as customers. You may be able to determine that by analyzing their advertising and social media. Have they changed their advertising recently? Do they seem to be targeting a new audience with their online marketing?

Demographics
What are the ages of the customers? Do they buy directly from the prospect in a store or online? Or do they purchase through a channel partner? In some cases, your prospect may target consumers who live within 10 miles of their physical stores. Other buyers will order a product online and expect it to be shipped across the country.

Psychographics
Understand how your prospect's products impact their customers. Are their customers excited about buying eyewear because the prospect donates to a related charity after each sale? Or are customers resigned to buying those products, think

motor oil) because their vehicles won't run without them? Customers' attitudes about what your prospect sells could provide an opening for you to change the business.

Additional psychographic research will tell you about the lifestyles of your prospect's customers. If your prospect is selling to young time-pressed parents, they may be able to increase revenue from quick-serve food regardless of how health oriented those customers are. When your prospects understand how their customers spend their free time, they'll be able to devise loyalty programs that speak to consumer wants and drive sales.

Shopographics

The company's advertising can also reveal whether they are pushing one product or brand over another. If they are running more promotional campaigns, has that activity coincided with a new product launch? Do the company's ads feature a shift in brand messaging?

Your online research, especially into public company financial statements or annual reports, may also reveal what percentage of the prospect's revenue comes from each customer type. That kind of information will help you properly position your solution when you contact the prospect.

Study your prospect's industry online, and dig into their website to understand how customers decide to buy their products and services in general. Do most customers find out about your prospect through specific sites online?

Tip: What other companies do your prospect's target customers consider when they're preparing to make a purchase? Those companies are your prospect's competition. The sales professionals who sell to those companies are your competitors. Adding that intelligence to your knowledge base allows you to speak authoritatively about who's who in the industry.

The purchasing patterns of a buyer's customers can also be useful intelligence. Are they buying the prospect's product every week? How much do they spend on the product or service? When you have that information, your credibility increases. Why? Because you might be able to talk with your buyer about price elasticity. If you mention that a 10% price increase on their top product will cut their customer base by 3%, they'll be worried. But if your solution adds value to the product in the eyes of their customers and they're willing to buy more, your prospect will want to hear more.

Another factor to be mindful of is the current state of the geographic markets where those customers live. Find out whether the local economy is booming or struggling. Is it driven by agriculture, a large university, or a manufacturing plant? Is the weather adversely impacting consumers in the market and therefore, your prospect?

Potential New Customers

In addition to knowing your buyer's customers, you should have intelligence about their noncustomers. Those noncustomers may be doing business with your buyer's competitors. How much is your buyer willing to spend to increase their market share?

Finally, know what your buyer's customers say about them. Reviews speak volumes about how your buyer is really doing. Do they have credibility in the marketplace? Check out sites like the Better Business Bureau, Yelp, and Facebook. You may be able to turn up information that your prospect doesn't yet have. Leading edge business leaders should always be concerned about customer comments.

1. Company

2. Contacts

3. Connections

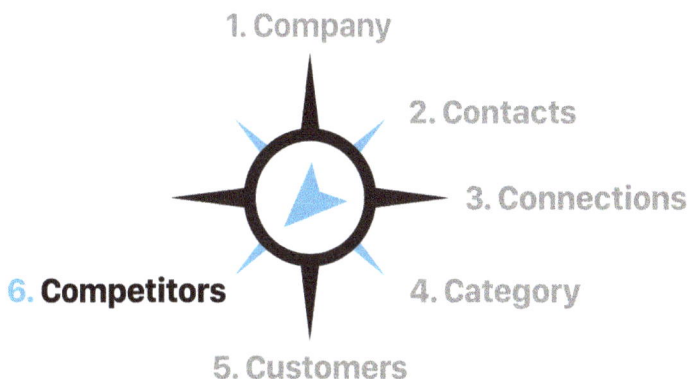

6. **Competitors**

4. Category

5. Customers

6. COMPETITORS

Competitive intelligence is a must for every business. Without this information, a business may end up launching a product into a crowded marketplace and struggle to grow sales. A lack of good industry information can cause a business to fail because the leadership hasn't realized that two former competitors have merged and can now more profitably sell their products at a lower price.

The marketplace is never stagnant. Businesses will always be gunning for your prospect's market share. A large conglomerate may launch a new product that directly targets your prospect's customers. A local business may also launch a new product or service that threatens your buyer's main line of business.

If your prospect hasn't been tracking these developments, it may take them several months to regain their momentum after a competitor makes a move. Imagine the credibility you'll build if you give your prospect a heads-up before that competitive product hits the market.

You can pick up some of that market intelligence by maintaining an extensive network of industry contacts. Chatting informally with those contacts at conferences in person can yield great tips. Check out online sites, such as G2 Crowd, that are devoted to venture capital news. Organizations that recently received a big round of funding will spend more to test and develop new products.

In the current business climate, many competitors have experienced serious drops in their revenue streams. Having that information shows your credibility as a sales professional. As you interact with your buyers, encourage them to go after the customers that their competitors have dropped.

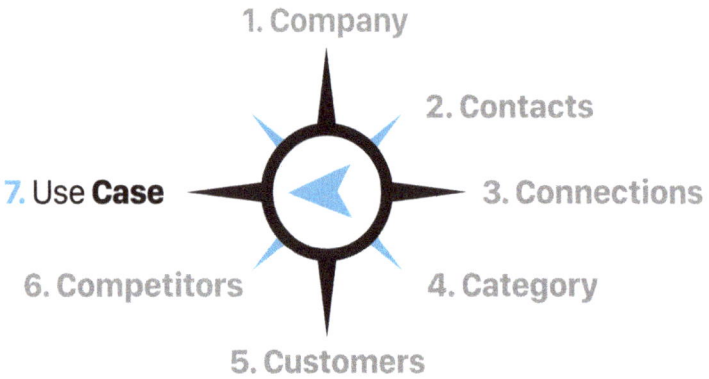

1. Company

2. Contacts

7. Use **Case**

3. Connections

6. Competitors

4. Category

5. Customers

7. USE CASE

With all the time you've spent developing your credibility in the eyes of your buyers and your target industry, you may wonder how you'll have time left for anything else. You know all about who is making and selling specific products and services, who's buying them, and where your prospects spend their free and professional time.

That intelligence won't do you much good unless you apply your solution to your buyer's needs when you first make contact. Use Case is the seventh C of credibility.

Tip: Our proprietary research shows that the top criterion that SMB buyers use when evaluating potential business partners centers on sales professionals who show how a solution will help them solve a problem.

To do that, you must maintain very high product knowledge and know the best features of your solution. Your creative thinking will help you show the buyer how they'll benefit when they do business with you.

Your proposal can't just state the ROI that the buyer will achieve if they choose you as a business partner. Consider the situation from their perspective. They're facing a big problem that potentially threatens their income stream. You've promised that you can help change their outcomes. But how will they get from Point A to Point B? That question will loom large in their decision-making process.

A highly credible salesperson will spell out the steps they'll take as they lead the buyer through the onboarding process and the use of their solution. Buyers must understand how to deploy products and services in the way that maximizes their revenue and profit. When that doesn't happen, they'll be quick to complain about you and your organization.

Take enough time to demonstrate how to use your product. Be prepared to explain who in the buyer's organization will use your solution. Show them how you will train and support those employees.

When you roll out the details for how your organization will onboard a buyer's employees, you'll sense the prospect starting to pay attention. That's because you're making their life easier. Not only will you handle the transfer from a legacy system, but you'll also offer outstanding support and provide a significant return on their investment.

At this point during a sales conversation, you're offering prospects inside information about your organization. They won't be able to obtain that intelligence by reviewing your corporate website. Once you present a use case, you've customized a solution for the buyer. Your credibility increases with every service promise you make.

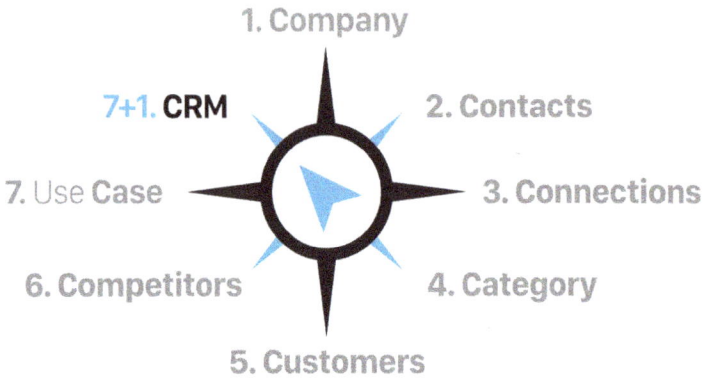

1. Company

7+1. **CRM**

2. **Contacts**

7. Use **Case**

3. **Connections**

6. **Competitors**

4. **Category**

5. **Customers**

7+1. CRM

One-third of SMB decision-makers say that sales reps who "don't take the time to learn about my business's past dealings with their company" are deal-breakers for them. Don't let that happen to you.

Your CRM can be your most effective tool when it comes to building your credibility. As you prospect and build your knowledge base on contacts in the target organization, your CRM should be your top resource. Another rep in your organization may have collected intelligence on one of your key contacts. Review that information to determine whether the contact has done business with your company before. If another sales rep in your company has called on the contact, talk with them to get additional information.

Review the database to determine what the company bought and what they didn't buy. How long ago did the sale and pitching activity occur? If the buyer ceased doing business with you for a particular reason, be prepared to address that topic. Explain how doing business with you this time will generate a positive outcome for them.

There's no better resource than a properly maintained CRM when it comes to account management. If you're trying to sell a solution to an existing account, take the time to learn the history of your company's business relationship with them. How long has it been since a rep in your organization has reached out to them? When was the last time the buyer purchased something from your company? Review what they bought and why they bought it. If nobody followed up to determine whether the buyer achieved the results they wanted because of the purchase, your first outreach to them should address that topic.

OTHER TOOLS AND RESOURCES
We've talked about tapping online resources to carry out your research. While your CRM will be a data-rich environment, your research shouldn't stop there. Which other resources will be most useful? Where should you start? Here are a few suggestions.

LinkedIn
LinkedIn will likely be one of your most valuable tools. Use LinkedIn to connect with target prospects and research their companies and their backgrounds. This tool also contains good intelligence on who has recently changed jobs in the industry.

Before you reach out to others, review your profile. How do you look on a credibility scale? Do you have enough connections? Enough connections means more than thirty. Is your college and volunteer organization information up to date? Remember to update your profile when you acquire a new skill.

Stay active on this site. You should be regularly sharing articles that you know will be of interest to leaders in your target industry, and you should be commenting on articles that others share.

Trade Associations and Publications
Subscribe to and regularly read the content on trade organization and association websites that support your buyer's line of business. Whether they sell software-as-a-service or aircraft engine parts, your ability to speak intelligently about the industry will directly impact your credibility. If you don't have time to read the material, listen to podcasts.

Proprietary Databases
Proprietary databases will give you a competitive edge that other salespeople won't have. Databases such as SalesCred PRO and AdMall® contain intelligence about the business category and customers that you must have. Other subscription-based data sources include ZoomInfo, SalesIntel, LinkedIn Sales Navigator, and Dun & Bradstreet.

In particular, those databases will outline in concise terms the SWOT of each business. When you understand a business's strengths, weaknesses, opportunities, and threats on a national and local level, people will listen.

To comprehend what drives consumers to purchase your buyer's products, turn to AudienceSCAN®. The profiles in that database will show you the media formats that influence buyers, the other products and services they intend to purchase in the next year, and how they spend their free time.

SUMMARY

As you've reviewed the discussion points covered in this section, you may have been telling yourself that you don't have time to commit to that level of pre-call research. We believe that you can't afford to skip any of these steps. If you want to feel confident about crushing your next sales goal, you must possess key intelligence that your competitors don't have. Your in-depth research will allow you to ask smarter discovery questions and see opportunities that other reps will miss.

With your increased credibility, you'll get access to sensitive business information that you can use to strengthen your bond with the buyer. You'll be able to decipher BS from a reticent prospect and overcome objections more easily. Your command of the 7 C's will ultimately allow you to close more deals.

Appendix

Salespeople are considered to be among the least credible professionals in America. This needs to change.

Credibility—and whether a person has it or not—determines whom you trust for guidance and which information you use to make decisions in your everyday life. The three pillars of credibility for any human being are being known, being likable, and being trustworthy. Credibility is gained (or lost) by what they say, how they say it, what they do, and finally, what others say about them.

Q: Do you agree or disagree that these professionals tend to be credible in what they say and do?

	Agree or Strongly Agree	Neither Agree nor Disagree	Disagree or Strongly Disagree
Nurses	81%	14%	4%
Doctors	78%	15%	7%
Pharmacists	77%	19%	5%
Small business owners	67%	27%	6%
High school teachers	66%	24%	9%
Weather forecasters	62%	28%	10%
College professors	60%	27%	13%
Accountants	57%	33%	9%
Hair stylists	57%	34%	9%
Nerds/geeks	57%	35%	9%
High-ranking military officers	55%	30%	15%
Judges	55%	29%	15%
Police officers	55%	24%	21%
Book authors	51%	39%	9%
State and federal public health directors	49%	28%	24%

	Agree or Strongly Agree	Neither Agree nor Disagree	Disagree or Strongly Disagree
Financial advisors	48%	36%	16%
Sports team coaches	46%	36%	18%
Religious leaders	46%	30%	24%
Local TV/radio/newspaper reporters	44%	30%	25%
Bartenders	43%	41%	16%
National news media reporters	37%	26%	37%
Business consultants	37%	43%	21%
Local government officials	36%	31%	33%
Home repair contractors	36%	38%	26%
Real estate agents	**35%**	**40%**	**25%**
Talk show/Podcast hosts	34%	38%	28%
Lawyers	34%	34%	32%
Business executives (other than CEOs)	30%	39%	31%
CEOs of publicly traded companies	29%	37%	34%
Salespeople (not automotive)	**28%**	**42%**	**30%**
Members of Congress	23%	27%	50%
Car salespeople	**20%**	**29%**	**51%**
	CREDIBLE	NEUTRAL	DUBIOUS

EXTRA POINT: Approximately 47% of Americans believe that most people have become somewhat or noticeably less credible in the previous year.

SOURCE: The American State of Credibility 2020, September 2020, Credibility Nation, SalesFuel and Behavioral Resource Group. Based on a representative sample of 1,025 online adults in the United States.

To inquire about the latest findings, visit salescred.com

When consumers buy a new car/truck, the dealership's credibility plays a key role in the purchase decision.

Q: What factors are most important to you when choosing a DEALERSHIP? (Check all that have a significant impact on your buying process)

1. Dealer reputation (48%)
2. Willingness to deal/negotiate fairly (43%)
3. Selection of vehicles available (38%)
4. Location close to home or work (34%)
5. Previous purchase experience—yours or someone you know (30%)

EXTRA POINT: Approximately 24% of auto buyers choose a dealership (in part) based on "where the salespeople are helpful and friendly."

SOURCE: AudienceSCAN 2020, March-April 2020, SalesFuel. Based on a representative sample of 15,281 online adults in the United States.

To inquire about the latest findings, visit AudienceSCAN.com

All these factors are important when an SMB decision-maker qualifies a seller. Some factors are more important than others.

Q: What are the top five attributes you seek in a salesperson who calls on you (top ten results shown)?

1. Knows their product (60%)
2. Provides relevant ideas to help my business (45%)
3. Is responsive (39%)
4. Is professional in conduct and appearance (51%)
5. Knows my company/line of business (44%)
6. Is experienced (42%)
7. Cares about me and my business (40%)
8. Delivers what they promise (39%)
9. Knows my customers (38%)
10. Is creative (32%)

EXTRA POINT: Nearly 30% of SMB decision-makers say that they are "willing to pay a premium to buy from a supplier that provides extra customer service."

SOURCE: Selling to SMBs Study, January 2019, SalesFuel. Based on an online sample of 1,166 self-reported owners, CEOs, other C-level executives, or purchasing agents of B2B companies with between 20 and 500 employees in the United States.

When buyers research what the internet says about you, they use very specific metrics to qualify or disqualify you.

Q: When researching a salesperson before I meet with them, I usually look for . . .
(Check all that apply.)

1. Years of experience (44%)
2. Length of time in previous jobs (31%)
3. Number of years in our industry (34%)
4. Names of previous employers (28%)
5. Their LinkedIn profile (27%)
6. Educational background (27%)
7. Their name in a Google search (24%)
8. Their posts on social media (24%)
9. Photographs they've taken (21%)
10. Articles they've written (21%)
11. Certifications (20%)
12. Their headshot/profile photo (19%)
13. Awards they've won (17%)

EXTRA POINT: Reviewing photographs posted on social media is most common among millennials.

SOURCE: Selling to SMBs Study, February-March 2019, SalesFuel. Based on an online sample of 1,166 self-reported owners, CEOs, other C-level executives, or purchasing agents of B2B companies with between 20 and 500 employees in the United States.

To inquire about the latest findings, visit https://salesfuel.com/selling-to-smbs

Exhibit any of these behaviors once, and you've disqualified yourself from the sale with many SMB decision-makers.

Q: Which of these salesperson behaviors are deal-breakers for you? (Check all that apply.)

1. Pushing me to make a decision I'm not comfortable making yet (39%)
2. Blaming other people for mistakes that were likely theirs (38%)
3. Sharing information that they've been asked not to (36%)
4. Having poor hygiene (36%)
5. Being arrogant or overconfident (35%)
6. Not returning my calls or emails (35%)
7. Having poor etiquette/manners/social skills (35%)
8. Being caught telling an obvious lie (34%)
9. Routinely being late (33%)
10. Treating my support staff poorly (33%)
11. Not taking the time to learn about my business' past dealings with the sales rep's company (33%)
12. Sharing confidential information from other sources (32%)
13. Dressing inappropriately or unprofessionally (32%)
14. Failing to deliver on their promises without my intervention (32%)
15. Treating me like I'm small potatoes (32%)
16. Talking too much about how great their products are instead of what they can do for me (30%)
17. Cussing/Using profanity (29%)
18. Badmouthing competitors (28%)
19. Behaving in a manner that conflicts with my personal beliefs (28%)
20. Making claims that may be truthful but are one-sided or exaggerated (23%)
21. Citing research that is misleading or from questionable sources (21%)
22. Wearing too much cologne or perfume (17%)

SOURCE: Selling to SMBs Study, February-March 2019, SalesFuel. Based on an online sample of 1,166 self-reported owners, CEOs, other C-level executives, or purchasing agents of B2B companies with between 20 and 500 employees in the United States.

To inquire about the latest findings, visit https://salesfuel.com/selling-to-smbs

There are key marketing offers and content that activate an SMB buyer to raise their hand as a prospect.

Q: What content influences you to share your contact information with a seller?

1. Provider customizes content to my needs (41%).
2. Provider offers insight on use of product/service to solve business problems (39%).
3. Provider offers primary research relevant to my business (37%).
4. Provider's online profile (34%).
5. Provider offers how-to tips (28%).
6. Provider maintains information on emerging market trends (26%).
7. Provider offers a free trial (25%).
8. Provider offers case studies and success stories (24%).
9. Provider offers an email newsletter subscription (10%).

EXTRA POINT: Approximately 28% say that a testimonial from a satisfied customer can influence their buying decision if it seems credible.

SOURCE: Selling to SMBs Study, February-March 2019, SalesFuel. Based on an online sample of 1,166 self-reported owners, CEOs, other C-level executives, or purchasing agents of B2B companies with between 20 and 500 employees in the United States.

To inquire about the latest findings, visit https://salesfuel.com/selling-to-smbs

It takes more than a good script to get a response when cold calling.

Q: What factors influence you to return a call or email from a salesperson you've never worked with before? (Check all that apply.)

1. Current or future need for a product or service (52%)
2. Seller has shared something of value (42%)
3. A referral from a co-worker (32%)
4. A referral from someone outside my company (31%)
5. Seller or company featured in an interview I saw/heard/read (30%)
6. Unhappy with my current provider (21%)

SOURCE: Selling to SMBs Study, February-March 2019, SalesFuel. Based on an online sample of 1,166 self-reported owners, CEOs, other C-level executives, or purchasing agents of B2B companies with between 20 and 500 employees in the United States.

To inquire about the latest findings, visit https://salesfuel.com/selling-to-smbs

Most sales reps don't even do the minimum amount of pre-call preparation to be perceived as credible resources.

Q: For the majority of sales calls, which activities do you perform for pre-call preparation? (Check all that apply.)

1. Review the company's website (52%).
2. Get up to date on developments in the prospect's industry (39%).
3. Check the company's account status with us (38%).
4. Talk to a contact inside the company (38%).
5. Study the company's target geographical market (37%).
6. Review my CRM notes/past activities (35%).
7. Study the latest developments in their industry (31%).
8. Research their competitors' latest developments (31%).
9. Prepare discovery questions based on pre-call research (31%).
10. Review the company's reputation, ratings, and reviews (30%).
11. Research the needs/tendencies of their ideal customers (29%).
12. Conduct a Google news search (27%).
13. Read the company's blog if they have one (24%).

SOURCE: Voice of the Sales Rep Study, February 2020, SalesFuel. Based on an online sample of 1,075 self-reported sales representatives in the United States.
To inquire about the latest findings, visit https://salesfuel.com/voice-of-the-sales-rep

About the Author

C. Lee Smith is the Sales Credibility Expert. For more than thirty years, he has helped salespeople leverage critical insights that enable them to acquire, develop, and retain their best customers by building their professional credibility in what they say and do every day.

He is the CEO and founder of SalesFuel®, a sales intelligence firm that has been recognized as one of the Top 10 Sales Enablement providers worldwide by *Selling Power* magazine.

Lee is one of a select few certified advisors worldwide for sales consultant Jeffrey Gitomer and was personally recognized as one of the Leading Sales Consultants by *Selling Power* magazine.

In addition to being a bestselling author and popular keynote speaker, he is also a C-Suite Network Advisor for sales leadership and co-host of the popular *Manage Smarter*™ podcast.

Lee is the creator of AdMall®, the leading sales intelligence platform for local media sales and digital marketing professionals. He is also the creator of the SalesFuel HIRE and SalesFuel COACH SaaS platforms for hiring and coaching your best sales talent.

He is also a certified professional behavioral analyst with expertise in consumer behavior, as well as the destructive impact that toxic employees have on your sales team.

Lee is a graduate of Ohio University, with a certificate in executive leadership from Cornell University.

When he's not in the office, Lee can be found on his bike, riding with his peloton, The Honey Badgers, and crushing long-distance rides to raise money for cancer research.

THiNKaha has created AHAthat for you to share content from this book.

- ⮑ Share each AHA message socially: **https://aha.pub/SalesCred**
- ⮑ Share additional content: **https://AHAthat.com**
- ⮑ Info on authoring: **https://AHAthat.com/Author**

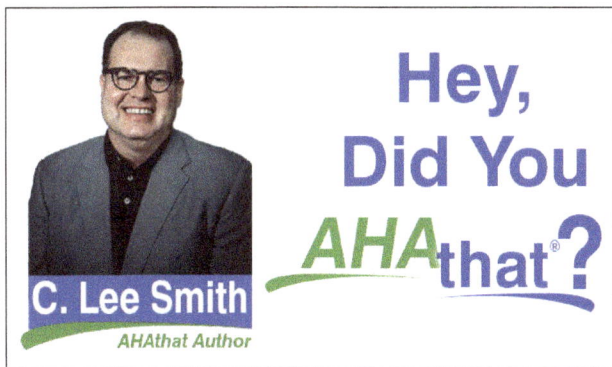

www.ingramcontent.com/pod-product-compliance
Lightning Source LLC
Chambersburg PA
CBHW042117190326
41519CB00030B/7531